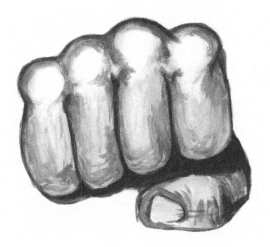

Steven Bruce

WHITE KNUCKLE

1987 Books

This paperback edition published 2020
by 1987 Books

1987books.info@gmail.com

First Edition

The right of Steven Bruce to be identified as the author of
this work has been asserted in accordance with section 77
of the Copyright, Designs and Patents Act 1988

A CIP record of this book
is available from the British Library

ISBN: 978-1-8380885-0-7

Cover illustration: White Knuckle, *acrylic on paper,
by Malgorzata Bruce, 2019*

AWARDS & NOMINATIONS

Winner of the Literary Titan Gold Book Award

Recipient of the Indies Today Five-Star Recommendation Badge

Runner-up for the Indies Today Poetry Book Award

Finalist for the Wishing Shelf Non-fiction Book Award

Shortlisted for the International Poetry Book Award

For my abusers,
who failed to break me.

CONTENTS

Contents

It's unfortunate that this has happened.

No. It's fortunate that this has happened
and I've remained unharmed by it.

— MARCUS AURELIUS ANTONINUS

WHITE KNUCKLE

Nursing

Pushed from the womb.

Into rat-infested squalor.
Where the lights didn't burn
and the water didn't flow.

Into drug and domestic abuse.
Where father held fire under the spoon,
and mother wept through bruised eyes.

Into physical and emotional abuse.
Where beatings broke the skin,
and we suffered piss-taking daily.

Into sleeping rough and foster care.
Where nights ached with unrest,
and foster houses were never home.

Sometimes we are hurled towards the tit,

and the breast milk we swallow
is rotten.

But we need it.

It makes us
grow.

A Domestic Song

At night it would rise up
through the floorboards.

Raised voices, vicious words,
the dog barking, then yelping,

scuffling, wailing, furniture
breaking, police sirens,

pounding on the front door,
neighbours gossiping in the street.

It was all part of the madhouse symphony.

A Domestic Dance

Their routine begins
like this:

Standing with precarious
posture, hands thrust
together.

They struggle, drag
each other around
the room.

She improvises, drives
a knee into his thigh,
they separate.

He grabs a handful of hair,
forces a bow, throws
a fist at her spine.

She twirls free, leaps
onto him, scratches
his tattooed face.

He throws her into the air
and doesn't bother catching her.

She crash-lands, sees me watching,
and declares they're not fighting,

only dancing.

Heat

I remember,
the morning was hot.

Standing idle in the kitchen,
chewing on a red sauce sandwich,
watching the dog eat sausage meat.

He burst in, claiming I'd stolen money
from his coat pocket.

With no chance to reply, two punches
to the head, and the dog ripped
into my foot.

I remember,
bleeding and crying and sweating
in the anxious fever of a typical day.

Knock-Knock

Both elbows on the kitchen table, palms
pressed into my face. Cardboard covers
up the broken window.

Mother snores on the couch, as usual,
it's mid-day. My brother scoops spaghetti
from the tin.

A knock arrives at the front door.

Stevie, my mother says, half-awake.
Tell them I'm not in.

I open the door, receive the simpers
of the god squad.

Is your Mother or Father in?
No, I say. *You'll have to come back later.*

I close the door and return to the kitchen.
My brother's tearful, holding his hand,
he shows me a cut on his finger.

I suck away the sauce and the blood,
run his wound under cold water.

Mother appears behind us.

For fuck's sake, she says.
You're meant to be watching him.

She sends me up to bed.

For part of the afternoon,
I lie wondering if the god squad
would come back.

They never did.

Hunger

Stale cream crackers, half a bottle of malt vinegar
in the kitchen cupboard, try making a meal out
of that.

Meanwhile, in the living room, mother tells
the social worker she needs money to replace

the broken

cooker and the kids need new clothes and bedding.
The social worker says she will get her the money
by tomorrow.

Months pass, we have the same worn-out clothes
and bedding and broken, grease-coated cooker.

The money dissolved in a spoon's bubbling eye.

From a Bathtub

Four inches of lukewarm water,
I clean my body with cheap
washing-up liquid.

Careful of the bruises, the cuts,
the blister on my bony chest.

Blood from a gash in my head runs
down into the brown water.

Someday these wounds will heal,
but for now, all you understand
is the bleeding.

Nineteen Ninety-Somethin'

The taste of stale smoke
hangs on in the living room.

My mother sits on the couch
alongside a wasted stranger.

She tells me she loves this man.

This man, who couldn't handle
his booze, a job, his temper.

Mother, you classic fool,
frittering your love away
on a man who brought you pills

instead of flowers.

You should have saved
a handful for yourself.

You might have burned on
instead of blazing out.

Toast

I
remember
making toast

on the gas fire.

Sticking
the fork
into a slice
of sour-smelling
bread
and holding it
to the heat.

The cheap
white bread
browning
quick.

Breakfast
served
without spreads,

a dry bite
of existence.

A Small Measure of Peace

When she came out of the hospital,
she made overcooked potato waffles,
gave me a cup of tap water, and a kiss
on the head. I didn't ask her about
the bandages around her wrists.

It was calm outside, calm inside.

The bloke she was seeing had stormed
off in a strop. We had food in out bellies,
no threat of violence, and a garden full
of tall grass, in which you could disappear,
if only for a moment.

At the Speed of Light

They poison their minds with alcohol, mother,
and her two friends. It's a school night,
we are up beyond midnight.

All of us huddled together in the lightbulb's
dreary glow, close enough to breathe
in their booze-stained lives.

Jock opens the bottle, swallows a mouthful,
gives it to Angela, swallows a mouthful,
gives it to my mother, swallows a mouthful.

Jock sparks up a joint, takes a few drags,
gives it to Angela, takes a few drags,
gives it to my mother, takes a few drags.

Jock insults Angela. Angela insults Jock.
He jumps up, splits her eyebrow
open with his boot.

And the drinking, arguments,
intoxicated blood
trickle on towards sunrise.

Parentification

She sparked up
a cigarette,
slouched back
into the couch,
slurred something.

All I could understand
was the last three words,

                               Love you, son.

Her eyes shut
and the cigarette
in her limp hand
sank towards
the cushion.

I took it from her
and stubbed it out
in the ashtray.

It was a regular Sunday morning.

A cartoon frolicked on the television
while we continued to star in reality.

About My Father

The doctor said he was
an old-fashioned psychopath.

Said he doused a policeman
in turpentine and tried to set
him alight.

I can believe this.

I once saw him stick a short blade
into my mother.

As a child, he suffered abuse,

My grandmother said she spoiled
him rotten.

The Adults Here Are Ornamental

Half-past-eight in the morning.
I should be making my way to school,
instead of standing between pensioners
in the Post Office queue.

The clerk stamps the benefit book
and counts out the money that fuels
my mother's drug problem.

When I return, the man of the house
is couch-bound watching TV.

It occurs to me that I spend my days
hand-washing clothes in the bathtub,
conjuring meals, cleaning the house,
wiping sick from my mother's mouth,

and at night,
I read my own bedtime stories.

The Last Visit

Christmas slips by without much ado.
Tangy tangerines, bland peanuts,
a second-hand figure
from the flea market.

In February, grandparents arrive,
unannounced, pass me a photograph
of my sister beaming inside
a circle of unopened presents.

They don't stay long, about an hour,
and before departure, they take back
the photograph, leaving us a handful
of nothing.

King of Inconvenience

When you're whacked on the head
with the handle of a hammer
ten times in a row,

lashed on the leg with a wet towel
until a stream of blood runs off
towards your heel,

get a slap, a punch, a kick in the gut,
splashed with boiling kettle water,
you know you exist.

The fire never lets you forget.

When you build up the courage
to tell family, teachers, neighbours,
and have the wounds to prove it,

your brave words forge
an awkward crown
of silence.

Deeper Than Flesh

Our scars are a testament
that we arrived at the battle.

View from a Doorway

On the living room floor,
beyond the smashed
wine
bottle
bits,
the ashtray crammed with cigarette ends,
the empty brown pill bottles,
the cream and blood-spotted rug,
the dented lampshade,
lies a sealed blue envelope

signed:

Happy birthday, son.

The Funeral

In church,
perched on a wooden bench,
front row.

Looking at the pictures
on colourful windows.

That musty church smell
clawing at my nostrils.

The standing, sitting, standing, sitting.

Mumbling along to songs
I didn't know the words to.

I still don't know the words to.
My mother, sobbing.

Feeling guilt
because I couldn't cry
for the man in the coffin.

That guilt, now long gone.

How could anyone feel anything
for an absent father?

White Knuckle

How tight they cling to their addictions,
knuckle moons, enough to lose hold
of their children.

Rodent

Between midnight and daybreak,
the sound of one rodent scratching
on floorboards.

I am expected to kill it,
as the adults always do.

This small thing that,
like me,
scurries this dangerous space,
hopes to discover a place
of salvation.

Does She Dig for Bones on the Other Side?

Joyriders strike a stray dog
down and leave her to bleed
out on the road.

My neighbour covers the mangled
parts with an old blanket.

I place a hand on her side,
attempt to soothe her hectic
breaths.

I tell her it's okay,
even though it isn't.

Her glassy eyes glare out at nothing.
The last frantic breath evaporates
into the night.

She slips the mortal collar,
on to the other darkness.

And now she knows,

more than me,
more than my neighbour,
more than you.

Colony

At night the hostel beds are full
of beaten mothers and their children.

We sleep, stinking of scabies lotion,
in a shoebox room.

A piss-head father stumbles from the midnight
silence, pounds on the front door,

yells he'll kill us all when he gets in.

We panic, hurry, double-check the locked
windows and doors.

The mothers find weapons,
await this drunken hornet.

I don't fancy his chances,
at all.

Shifting

Her weed rolled out to whizz.
Her whizz flowed on to heroin.
Her heroin ebbed to methadone,

    for a while.

Her methadone rushed on to heroin,
codeine, amitriptyline, and diazepam.

Her addiction swept her to suicide.
Her death left us stranded with a shark.

And on it goes,
one thing never the same.

Like the tides,
we shift.

Finding

When we returned home
on a Saturday afternoon,
she was sprawled
out on the couch.

I called her, expecting
some movement.

I shook her shoulder,
stepped back.

I noticed the empty pill bottles.
I noticed the stillness of her face.
I noticed the piss she left behind.

They told me she'd be okay,
but I knew what happened.

She gave up on us.

She had enough of the circus.

Kiss

The last time I kissed
you is the coldest thing
I've known.

My fearful lips
pressed to your pallid
cheek

as you lay hushed
in the mortuary.

Family Valuables

My mother rests,
in the living room,
tucked up tight
inside of a cheap
coffin.

A handful of family
and friends
pick
at a pile
of dry
sandwiches
and sip
piss-weak
orange juice.

It all
still tastes
surreal.

She swallowed
enough pills
to be rid
of them.

Yet here they stand,
debating
on how to share
out her jewellery.

Not all vultures
have feathers.

But nobody
wants to take
her outstanding debts,
her blood-stained clothes,
her sweat-scented sheets,
her beat-up children.

Fetch
the small
jewellery box.

Reveal. Surprise.

Worthless
dust
and tin.

The looks
on their faces,
priceless.

Sand and Moonlight

Violence tears
through the house
with stitched-up
eyes.

Nothing is safe
except for the TV.

Hellhound,
find me first.

I will not flee.

Best to get it
over with.

My body understands
the shooting stars of agony.

How the bruises
mellow to yellow.

How the scars
linger to silver.

Tonight, I am your barren child

of sand
and moonlight.

When to Quit

This day, like many before,
we play his favourite game.

The one where I sit, hands-on-head,
legs out, back up straight.

He begins his part:
Let's see how long you last, eh, dickhead?
Fucking weirdo. No wonder you've got no friends.
Your own family doesn't even want you.
Your mother killed herself because of you.

It goes on like this,
and   on   like   this.

I'm not giving in this time, I tell myself.
So far, I'm winning. No fidgeting. No tears.

Time drags on, my shoulders burn numb,
my arms shake, my hands drop.

The swift punch lands
on the side of my head.

The game ends in another loss.
I realise I should give in sooner.

There's no victory for me here.

A Delayed Return Home

The final bell
of the day
signals the start
of the journey
back to my own
personal underworld.

Wander homeward,
muddy school trousers,
I will pay for this
when I get home.

On the street kerb,
a man downs vodka
from the bottle.

Walk by,
muddy school trousers,
I will pay for this
when I get home.

Two lovers argue
on their doorstep,
Fuck off, silly cunt, stupid slut.

Walk by,
muddy school trousers,
I will pay for this
when I get home.

Shoplifters
are shifting bacon,
batteries, and big
jars of coffee
on the cheap.

Walk by,
muddy school trousers,
I will pay for this
when I get home.

A ghoulish junkie
rushes towards
her next fix.
Sorry,
somebody's daughter
rushes towards
her next fix.

Walk by,
muddy school trousers,
I will pay for this
when I get home.

Careful of
where you step,
fresh dog shit lurks
amongst old garbage.

Walk by,
muddy school trousers,
I will pay for this
when I get home.

Black bonfire
smoke
spills out
into the street.
Neighbours toss
an old couch
onto the flames.

Walk by,
muddy school trousers,
I will pay for this
when I get home.

A hulking dog
rages
at the garden fence.
I pray
it doesn't leap
over.

Walk by,
muddy school trousers,
I will pay for this
when I get home.

A hop, skip, and a jump
over dirty, used
smack needles.

Walk by,
muddy school trousers,
I will pay for this
when I get home.

My friend
waves to me
from his broken
window.

Next week,
he will be
dead.

Walk by,
muddy school trousers,
I will pay for this
when I get home.

A police car
parked outside
of number 16.
Bigger kids jam
nails under the tyres
and scarper.

Walk by,
muddy school trousers,
I pay for this
when I get home.

Boiled

Run it around the plate, mop up the burnt
spaghetti hoop sauce, shovel down the final
undercooked potato, dark eyes and all.

The night begins with a slow chew, a dull breath,
and a limp to the only place you never weep,

your sleep.

Alarm

At dawn,
you sleep beyond the call
to rise from slumber.

The alarm
creeps up to your room.

His first hand slams into your face,
the second drags you up, marches
you over the landing, throws you
down the last couple of stairs.

You stand, dazed, stagger
into the kitchen, and sit
down to a breakfast
of warm sanguine
fluid.

Unacknowledged

The silence, broken
by a smack across the lips.

Accusations of stealing food
are met with blood-covered
words of innocence.

The silence, broken
by a rumbling in the gut.

And ligature marks
on your neck
from a failed suicide
go by unacknowledged.

Pinch

Kicked out,
at fourteen-years-old,
I was half-glad.

They said I smoked marijuana.
True.
They said I associated with undesirables.
True.

The first night homeless,
drifting off under the open sky,
I was free enough to smile.

The first morning homeless,
the cold nipping at my bones.

my eyes open
to the clatter of a milk float
crossing a pothole.

It stops. I rise,

lift a pint,
and return to the cover
of a dark
blue morning.

Black Dog

Waking up in the claws
of a frigid morning,
on a rusty
graveyard
bench.

This black dog
resting at my side.

A bloke
wanders
into view.

Did you sleep out here, kid?
        Yeah, I say, *and?*
You'll get pneumonia, he says.

        I couldn't give a fuck.

The bloke
walks off.

The black dog
stays with me.

Restless

Night possesses
the graveyard.

Hunger haunts
this gaunt gut.

Wind rattles
my juvenile bones.

Raw lips buried
beneath my shirt,

confessing to the dead,
I want to be one of you.

Sleep

I've slept intoxicated in the womb.
I've slept in a squat, as an infant and teenager.
I've slept in a hostel for battered mothers.
I've slept with bruised ribs and bloody lips.
I've slept, restless, after finding my mother's suicide.
I've slept in the back of a car and under a caravan.
I've slept with split knuckles in a piss-stained alley.
I've slept on the steps of a boarded-up house.
I've slept with a three-day hunger.
I've slept beneath a bridge, with a knife wound.
I've slept as an alienated teenager in foster care.
I've slept in a cell, stinking of cheap weed.
I've slept on bare breasts and thighs.
I've slept on wet grass.

And one day,
I'll sleep beneath it.

Cars

Waiting
to cross a busy road
in the bowels of a hot
day.

The cars flash-by and don't give way.

Realise that all you have to lose
in this cut-throat world
is the ragged clothes on your back.

The cars flash-by and don't give way.

Realise that if you stepped out
into the road, a car
would mangle you into oblivion.

The cars flash-by and don't give way.

Realise that the only person who
would lose any sleep,
is the hapless bastard that hit you.

The cars flash-by and don't give way.

Realise that in another life,
you may have been worthy of something,
dare I say loved.

Failing

Wandering the deserted streets at dawn
with dirty skin, no food for three days.

Feet blistered from wet, worn-out shoes,
knuckles grazed from fighting off two junkies.

Elbow stinging from a weeping knife wound,
I retire under the railway bridge.

School report card tucked inside my pocket,
it says I must try harder.

Street Gum

The stars have beaten
dusk out of town.

I am alone with a hot
bottle of vodka,

watching the full moon
from the cracks

of the pavement.
It looks like I feel,

chewed up,
spat out,

trampled flat
like street gum.

Wisdom from a Working Girl

In the late-night murmur of distant traffic,
lounging on a graffiti-stained wall,
at the corner of the street.

A gaunt woman approaches
wearing a blue tracksuit steeped
in cheap perfume.

Excuse me, she says. *Do you have a tab I could pinch?*
        No, I say. *I don't smoke.*
Good lad, she says. *What are you doing out this late?*
        Getting some air, I say. *What about you?*
I'm a working girl, she says.

I had to ask.

        How much do you charge?
Fifty for a blowjob, a hundred for full sex,
she says. *Are you interested?*

No offence, I say. *But I get it for free.*

A kerb crawler rolls up in a white car.

Nothing's free, she says and moves on
to have her holes and pockets filled.

A Need for New Shoes

Sitting in the hum of hot garbage,

I watch an older friend tie his bicep with string,
inject smack bought with the money
from yesterday's crimes.

He slides out of this diabolical reality,
leaving behind enough heroin for me.
But I want none of it.

This is how my idiotic father died.

Instead, I take my money to the corner shop,
buy a tuna sandwich, cheap deodorant,
and a cold fizzy drink.

On my way back to the squat
I hope for new shoes.

The ones I'm wearing now
are fucked.

Avocado

Most of my youth spent living in squats,
hostels, and rat-infested houses.

We ate from chipped plates, tins, and cartons
with dirty forks and fingers.

Most of the time, I ate alone.

The first night in foster care, sitting with three
strangers at their candlelit table.

The spotless cutlery.

Talk of work and laughter.
I sat, silent, hoping to blend in.

The starter was served, prawns with weird
green slices which, to me, seemed out of place.

For What Is Yours

I'd forgotten about the small
spider beside the fridge.

I'd planned on scooping it up
and tossing it out into the garden.

When I returned, I noticed
a larger spider face-to-face
with the small one.

Curiosity defeated me.

I left them alone for a few days,
to see what would happen.

When I looked again, the larger spider
was gone, and poised in the centre
of the web was the little guy.

He'd claimed his ground,
beaten the odds,

how could I throw him out
into the cold after that?

On Reflection

My parents left me
unprepared for the world.

For over twenty years
they have been ash
in a pot.

I am still fumbling
around in old wounds,

trying to make sense of it all.

If I understand anything,
it is that life doesn't come to you
with a trigger warning.

It leaps from the dark, bearing flowers,
a painted-on grin, and a short
sharp blade
to push up into your gut.

Verse for Midnight Rain

How important you are tonight,
for me, to hear your pitter-patter melody.

In this small room, this small town,
this small scratch of time.

At this desk, carving out
a poem about my mother's suicide,

my eyes compose silent notes.

How important you are tonight,
for me, to hear your pitter-patter melody.

In this small room, this small town,
this small scratch of time.

To understand,
you have come
to clear the air.

The Drum

Hope dried up
along with the eyes
of my dead mother.

The succeeding years
chiselled me as a cynic.

Yet, there are nights like this,
where the drum still pounds
and my blue soul marches.

Departure

I come from council estates, housemates
with vermin
and evil bastards. Dog shit gardens, smackhead
alleys,
coffee tables stacked with empty cider bottle
dreams.

We were underage, but we drank anyway.
We were underage, but we smoked anyway.
We were underage, but we fucked anyway.

I come from council estates, housemates
with vermin
and evil bastards. Mindless violence, bad
decisions,
police raids, a methadone kiss good
night.

I was a mistake or child benefit.

My friends became addicts.
My friends became suicide.
My friends became murder.

I remember the place that I come from,

but I'd have been a fool
to stay there.

Standpoint

We are not the ashes of our past,
but embers burning towards a future fire.

Dear Mother

I wasn't enough to make you stay.

When you left, I was a lace-thin boy with a dirty neck,
and couldn't do much, except roll your cigarettes.

Some afternoons, I would fetch your methadone,
we would watch cartoons with a jam sandwich.

Those are my best childhood memories.

When you left, I was a lace-thin boy with a dirty neck,
and couldn't do much, except roll your cigarettes.

The years have slipped by me.

I have ceased asking questions
that will never know answers.

The days that I blamed you
for leaving me in the hands
of a man that beat me up
for four-years straight
have gone.

From the embers
of my soul,
I can finally say,

Mother, I forgive you.

Letting Go

Strength comes,
not in the grip,

but the opening
of the hand.

A LETTER TO MY YOUNG SELF

A Letter to My Young Self

27th December 2019

Dear Stevie,

I'm writing this letter from a hotel room in Rome.
The weather today is glorious.

This morning at the Colosseum, I thought of you
and the battle you have on your little hands.
It is beyond shameful that you must face it alone.

Concede, your family are too busy pretending
not to notice your situation. It grieves me to say
that I can't help you either.

I'm twenty-two years away.

The only hands that will save you are your own.
And because nobody ever tells you this, I must.

Your life is worth saving.

Now, I could inundate you with cliché advice,
but what child in their right mind would listen?

Is it not enough to reveal that you survive, grow
from your mistakes, become resilient and learn
to be an independent thinker?

It may also encourage you to know
that life improves far beyond belief.

You graduate from university
with a Master's Degree, travel to France,
Andorra, Spain, Poland, Italy, Belgium,
Scotland, and the Netherlands.

So don't be too upset about the school trips
you miss out on and pay no attention to your
teachers, you *do* make something of yourself.

After a few years of drifting through uncertainty,
working dead-end jobs, you discover a passion
for writing poetry and short stories.

You will see your work published in magazines.

I know this is hard to believe, but you also find
a deep admiration for literature and understand
why reading is so invaluable to our lives.

Many great authors will inspire and humble you.

But best of all, you will fall in love
with the most incredible woman,
brave, ambitious, and independent.

You will marry and begin a loving life together.

So in the meantime, keep your guard up,
be patient, endure, and remember,

it is not what happens to you,
but how you react to it that matters.

With love, always,
Your Older Self

P.S. Know that I wish to change nothing.
It all contributed to where we are today.

ACKNOWLEDGEMENTS

Acknowledgements

"Nursing", "A Domestic Song", and "A Domestic Dance" first appeared in *The Black Light Engine Room Literary Magazine,* "The Drum", and "For What Is Yours" in *The World of Myth Magazine,* "Street Gum" in *No Tribal Dance International Anthology.*

Writing this collection opened many old wounds. I had to revisit traumatic experiences from the first sixteen years of my life and face up to some hard truths. But in doing so, I experienced a kind of cathartic liberation. Yet, it would have been a more formidable foe if not for the handful of great people in my life. I would especially like to thank my wife, Malgorzata, who has been an absolute pillar of stability, encouragement, and strength. Jason Matthews for his friendship which remains precious to me, for over a decade. Bob Beagrie, tutor, author, and friend for his invaluable guidance. Margaret Williams, author, artist, and friend for her continued support.

Finally, I would like to thank Frank O'Neill for his encouragement and creative writing class. Without it, this book would not have been written.

ABOUT THE AUTHOR

About the Author

Steven Bruce is a writer and multiple-award-winning author. His poems and short stories have appeared in numerous international anthologies and magazines. In 2018, he graduated from Teesside University with a Master's Degree in Creative Writing. He is the recipient of the Literary Titan Golden Book Award, the Firebird Book Award, and the Indies Today Five-star Recommendation Badge. An English expatriate, he now lives and writes full-time in Barcelona.

1987 Books | Author photograph, Madrid, 2019

INDEX OF FIRST LINES

Index of First Lines

Most of my youth spent living in squats 51
My mother rests in the living room 30
My parents left me unprepared for the world 53

Night possesses the graveyard 44

On the living room floor 21
On the street kerb, a man downs vodka 32
Our scars are a testament 20

Pushed from the womb 3

Run it around the plate, mop up the burnt 39

She sparked up a cigarette 15
Sitting in the hum of hot garbage 50
Stale cream crackers, half a bottle of malt vinegar 9
Strength comes 59

The doctor said he was 16
The final bell of the day 34
The last time I kissed you 29
The silence broken 41
The stars have beaten dusk out of town 48
The taste of stale smoke 11
Their routine begins 5
They poison their minds with alcohol 14
This day, like many before 33

1987
Books

To find out more about this author please visit
www.stevenbrucewriter.co.uk

For book details and other information email
1987books.info@gmail.com